# Mending Hearts: A Journey From Infidelity to Intimacy

Love You Series

Book 3

By Wyshina West

# OVERCOMING INFIDELITY

Discovering that your significant other has been unfaithful is one of the most devastating instances you'll experience in life. You may feel broken, ashamed, and even sick to your stomach.

You may decide to hibernate for weeks, while stewing about your partner's act of infidelity. Or, you may choose to ignore the news and continue on with your life as if nothing has happened.

It's important to understand that both are perfectly normal reactions. In fact, **_there's no right or wrong way to react to such devastating news._**

But at some point or another, you _will_ have to come to terms with what has happened. You'll have to find the will to dig yourself out of the emotional slump you're currently in.

Though you may not realize it at the moment, your hurt is only temporary. There will be calm after the storm.

And, if you're willing to take strides towards a future together, you and your partner can endure the healing process jointly as one.

# ACCEPTING WHAT HAS HAPPENED

Your partner has wronged you in the most hurtful way a lover can possibly fathom: *betrayal.* The fact that your partner has been unfaithful is never easy to accept. It's an especially tough pill to swallow if you were under the impression that your relationship was better than ever.

**There are two aspects to acceptance: mental and emotional.** Both are equally important in overcoming the effects of infidelity. But for the moment, let's zone in on the mental aspect of acceptance.

## The Mental Aspect

In order for your mind to fully accept that your partner has been unfaithful, you must set aside your emotions. It's important to understand that **there is logic behind every action, even one as foolish as infidelity.**

Most people believe that infidelity stems from sexual dissatisfaction. But, a lacking sex life isn't always to blame for an act of infidelity.

Infidelity typically stems from a lack of a *vital factor* in a romantic relationship. Below is a list of the 7 "lacks" that lead to infidelity.

# The 7 "Lacks" of Infidelity

1.  Lack of affection

2.  Lack of attention

3.  Lack of admiration

4.  Lack of sexual attention

5.  Lack of attraction

6.  Lack of excitement

7.  Lack of communication

The fact of the matter is that infidelity doesn't *"just happen."* No one wakes up one morning and thinks, "Hmm, I think today is a nice day to cheat on my spouse."

Your partner was unfaithful because your relationship lacked something that they found necessary.

As hard as it may be to hear, *infidelity is a byproduct of problems that have been stirring in your relationship* for months, perhaps even years. However, this is not to say that you are to blame, because you certainly aren't.

If your partner was dissatisfied with an aspect of your relationship, it was their responsibility to confess their worries. Your partner should've expressed such important concerns. Dropping subtle hints or acting out their frustration aren't effective ways of approaching marital or relationship problems.

Maybe you argue too often, maybe your lover is feeling belittled or ignored, or perhaps they're tired of the same old routine every day.

If you aren't planning on ending the relationship, the good news is that each of these culprits of infidelity can be turned around. But, you must be willing to work together.

Remember, it takes two people to build a relationship, but only one to tear it down.

Ask yourself: **Has your relationship changed recently (before the infidelity)?**

Before having a discussion with your partner about what happened, take a long look at your relationship. As previously mentioned, push your emotions to the side and think only in a factual state of mind.

Put yourself in your partner's mindset, and try to understand their reasoning.

Explore any and all weaknesses. Has your sex life drastically changed over the years? Have you stopped taking care of your appearance? Or, perhaps you've stopped paying your partner compliments that used to make their day.

In relationships, both men and women want to feel adored and as if they can trust their partner with their deepest darkest secrets.

If you feel that perhaps your partner isn't getting all of these things from you, you just may have found the reason for their infidelity. *It may not be a good reason,* but it might contribute to one of the "lacks" that they feel.

## The Emotional Aspect

Your heart is hurting. Your mind isn't at its best. And it feels as if the world is caving in on you. All of these feelings are perfectly normal and quite expected.

In fact, if you don't feel at least *one* of these symptoms even mildly, you likely aren't as emotionally attached to your partner as you'd like to think.

In such a painful time, you may want to be around family and friends. Though being with your loved ones may lessen the emotional impact of the infidelity, it might do little good otherwise.

Until you've talked things through with your partner, it's often best to spend time reflecting on your relationship by yourself for a few days. Surrounding yourself with the overwhelming advice and strong opinions of others may drive you towards making a decision you may later regret.

Take a few days to think about what has happened away from the distractions of others. Send your kids to grandma's house for a few days. And send your partner to a hotel, or at the very least, the guest room, until you've accepted the situation and thoughtfully determined your next step.

## Accept Your Emotions

*Allow yourself to feel the natural emotions spilling from your soul.* Trying to oppress them will only make them lie dormant for the time being. Then they'll eventually work their way to the surface and you'll experience them all over again.

Allow yourself to cry, scream, sulk, curse, and do anything else (within reason) that your emotions compel you to do. You'll feel better once all of the angst and depression is out of your system.

Let your emotions flow freely, and then pick the pieces back up in a day or two. *You'll make a more rational decision once your emotions have had their time to steal center stage.*

# Reflect on Your Relationship

In your time alone, reflect on your relationship. What are your partner's good traits? Where does he fall short? What has he recently done that made you smile? Make a list and check it twice.

Unfortunately, people often remain together due to a high level of comfort, not love. When you've been with someone for so long, it's easy to fall out of love and not even notice.

If you have nothing nice to say about your partner, you both may have neglected your relationship for far longer than you've imagined.

# COPING WITH YOUR PAIN

Whether you're planning on remaining with your partner or diving into the single life, coping with your pain is necessary in order to give yourself a fresh start.

There are productive and unproductive ways to deal with your pain. To clear the air, let's discuss the unproductive methods of coping with your pain.


## Unproductive Methods of Coping with Pain


- Drinking Alcohol

- Binging on food

- Chain smoking

- Taking drugs

- Hurting yourself

- Hurting your partner

It's true that everyone needs an outlet, but defaulting to unhealthy, dangerous and potentially life threatening methods of coping with your pain will do more harm than good.

Avoid drinking alcohol and taking drugs because you won't be in your right state of mind and may do something you may regret. Furthermore, by exposing yourself to these harmful indulgences, you risk becoming dependent on drugs and alcohol.

Though a bit of ice cream and chocolate does your achy heart some good, binging on junk food each day isn't a healthy outlet. Not only will you gain weight, but you're only masking the true problem.

Hurting anyone, including yourself, is unacceptable. Resulting to violence will only complicate the situation and leave you with plenty of regret.

Do yourself a favor and *be smart about the way you cope with your pain.* Preserve your life by writing off these excuses to sabotage yourself.

Now, let's discuss the productive methods of coping with

your pain.


## Productive Methods of Coping with Your Pain


- ◉    Consulting with a certified couple's therapist

- ◉    Attending spiritual retreats or church groups

- ◉    Seeking online forums dedicated to overcoming

infidelity

- ◉    Reading relevant books

- ◉    Journaling your feelings

- ◉    Confiding in a friend


*The best way to cope with your pain is seeking comfort from those who have gone through similar situations.* Perhaps you have a friend, family member, or coworker that has overcome infidelity. If so, contact them and ask them to tell you how they dealt with the situation.

Generally, people like telling their untold stories of hardship and will be honored that you've turned to them for help.

If you don't have a personal friend that can see you through this time, mingle online and in local organizations with those who can help. You'll often find forums online and local groups filled with members that are ready and willing to help you cope.

*Explore your options.* You can contact a professional, close friend, or a complete stranger online. The important thing is to get your feelings out into the open.

Alternatively, if you prefer to keep your partner's act of infidelity private, simply journal your feelings. *Journaling can help you express your emotions and think through different options.*

There's always someone ready to listen to your troubles, even if that someone is you.

# SEEING THE RELATIONSHIP THROUGH

Dealing with infidelity is one of the most trying situations a couple can encounter.

After the fact, there's only one of two roads which you can embark on. You can either try to forgive the betrayal and rebuild your relationship, or you can let the relationship go and start anew.

If you feel you must leave because you'll never be able to trust your partner again, you may wish to end the relationship. Such a decision should be made only *after* you can think rationally again, and hopefully after you and your partner have had ample chance to communicate with each other about the future.

Counseling may also help you arrive at a realistic decision for you.

No one will think any less of you because you could not

forgive and forget; many people do not possess the ability to let

something of such a large magnitude go.

However, if you do want to see the relationship through, it *is*

possible! You've invested love, time, and effort into this

relationship. It's well within your rights to want to protect your

investment!

## Rebuilding a Loving Relationship

Some days will be easier than others. All you can do is take

each day as it comes and keep your goal in mind: a harmonious

life with your partner.

In the beginning, you'll likely feel as if you must control your partner's every move in fear of them cheating again. It's important to resist this urge!

This is their chance to prove to you that they are worthy of your forgiveness. If they truly aspire to live their life beside you, no temptation in the world will be worth sacrificing your life together.

On the other hand, when a person truly wants to do something, they'll find a way to go about it. If your partner isn't in it for the long haul, your attempts to control them will do no good.

Rebuilding your relationship after infidelity is much like courting a new romance. You'll get to know each other again. You'll spend romantic evenings together. Each kiss will hold meaning and emotion. And your time together will be a priority, not an afterthought.

*This act of infidelity was a bump in the road.* If you're both willing to pour the necessary effort into rebuilding your love and trust, you *will* make it work.

## Couples Counseling

As mentioned above, couples counseling can be an effective remedy to mending your broken heart and strengthening your bond. Book an initial consultation with a reputable therapist and, if you're comfortable with their techniques, schedule a weekly counseling session.

In couple's counseling you'll be able *to tap into each other's most reserved feelings* and get to know each other all over again. Though couple's counseling is effective, it's also an expensive form of rekindling your romance.

If your finances are in good standing, go ahead and schedule a few sessions. However, if you're struggling financially, find out what your insurance covers and whether the counselor offers reduced rates based on income.

## Strengthening Your Relationship

Rev up your sex life by purchasing sexy lingerie or trying new techniques. Strengthen your bond by spending more quality time together. If possible, schedule daily lunches together or call each other on your lunch breaks. Small gestures go a long way.

**Here are 10 activities to rekindle the romance:**

1. Schedule a weekly date night.

2. Have dinner together *every* night.

3.      Sincerely compliment one another at least 5 times per day.

4.      Buy each other small, thoughtful gifts.

5.      Cook a home-cooked meal together.

6.      Treat each other to weekly massages.

7.      Have sex at least 3 times per week.

8.      Take romantic trips regularly.

9.      Visit the place where you had your first date or were proposed to.

10.     Have fun! Go to a concert, race, or romantic getaway.


By incorporating the activities listed above into your weekly routines, you just may feel like newlyweds again. All anyone wants is to love and to be loved. Nothing says *"I love you"* like having the spirit of an infatuated teenager and the bond of an 80-year old couple.

*__The only way to overcome infidelity is to truly re-dedicate__*
*__your life to one another.__* Your partner should be your main priority,
the reason you wake up every morning, and the person that makes
your heart flutter. Whether you've been married for 20 years or
have been dating for just 8 months, by taking it one step at a time,
you can successfully overcome infidelity.

Now that we have discussed some key points and ways to
overcome infidelity, let's dive into Intimacy and how to deepen it
in your relationship. We are mending hearts and healing today!
Part 2 begins on the next page.

# How to Deepen Intimacy in Your Relationship

*"When someone loves you, the way they talk about you is different. You feel safe and comfortable." – Jess C. Scott*

The rush felt at the start of a relationship is exciting and invigorating. You're going on dates, trying new things, getting to know someone new. Everything feels easy and energizes you.

But as the relationship progresses, things become more complicated. Those initial feelings naturally begin to fade, date nights happen less frequently, and misunderstandings happen.

When this happens, you might feel lost. After all, we don't learn how to handle the complexities of a relationship in school.

You might start wondering how you can continue getting closer with your partner once the initial excitement starts to fade. One trick is by deepening the intimacy in your relationship.

When you read the word "intimacy," you might instantly associate it with sex. **Intimacy is the closeness and connection you feel with someone else.**

Just like you can have sex without intimacy, you can have intimacy without sex. And there are different types of intimacy.

**In a relationship, intimacy is how you grow your love and desire for someone.**

Intimacy is the glue that keeps relationships together after the initial spark fades. Intimacy is a closeness that builds over time in a relationship. It is that safe space where you can be vulnerable and open.

It's being understood, letting your walls fall down, and being accepted.

Maintaining and growing intimacy takes work, intention and time. It will certainly benefit you to make it a priority.

Use these topics to deepen the intimacy of your relationship and get that ring:

- **The Importance of Intimacy in Relationships.** What are the types of intimacy?

- **10 Obstacles to Building Intimacy.** What are the obstacles that make building intimacy in your relationship more challenging? Here are the obstacles to avoid and what you can do to overcome them.

- **Self-Intimacy and its Impact on the Relationship.** How can your relationship with yourself deepen the connection in your romantic relationship? Having a truly intimate relationship with your beloved starts with the relationship with yourself first.

- **Building Trust and Intimacy.** Trust is the foundation for intimacy in your relationship. Couples will need to trust that each other's love is unconditional and that they can lean on each other for support.

- **Emotional Intimacy.** Emotional intimacy is how safe and secure you feel with your partner. It's built through raw, deeper conversations about feelings, struggles and needs.

- **Intellectual Intimacy.** Intellectual intimacy is getting to know how your partner's mind works. You learn about your partner's opinions and the way they see the world.

- **Building Physical Intimacy.** See how physical intimacy can boost your immune system, help you live longer, and keep you happier.

- **Experiential Intimacy.** Experiential intimacy is built by doing shared activities with your partner. It's growing your memory bank, creating inside jokes, and enjoying time together.

- **Building Intimacy Beyond Conflict.** Instead of settling when things get hard, the disagreements you have can become a way for you to understand each other better, learn, and grow. That's how you build intimacy beyond conflict.

- **5 Exercises to Build Intimacy.** These exercises will bring you closer together. Follow these practical tips in your daily life to feel understood in a way you haven't before.

If you apply what you learn in this section, it will affect you in wonderful ways.

# The Importance of Intimacy in Relationships

Although deepening intimacy is challenging and takes time, the work done will enhance the quality of your relationship and your life.

Intimacy is important because **it is the glue that helps a relationship get through difficult times.** Intimacy builds a safe space for honesty and openness. It creates opportunities for you and your partner to learn from each other and grow.

Your basic human desire to be understood can be fulfilled by intimacy.

**The closeness found in intimacy will create a safe space where you feel heard, accepted, and understood by your partner.**

As you get closer with your partner, you can develop four different types of intimacy.

**These are the different types of intimacy in relationships:**

1. **Emotional.** Emotional intimacy is building closeness and trust. It's that safe space you create to share your deepest thoughts and feelings with each other.

2. **Intellectual.** Intellectual intimacy is getting to know how your partner's mind works. Ideas, thoughts, and opinions. Accepting differences of opinions.

3. **Physical.** Physical intimacy is built through touch and physical closeness.

4. **Experiential.** Experiential intimacy is built by doing activities with your partner.

**A truly healthy relationship builds on all four of these types of intimacy.**

As you get closer to your partner, you might learn that you each have different intimacy styles.

What types of intimacy are most important to you? What types of intimacy are important to your partner? That type of intimacy style would be your intimacy language.

While you'll likely practice every intimacy style in your relationship, keep in mind which intimacy language your partner speaks.

## What You Need to Build Intimacy

**These are the essential ingredients to build intimacy:**

1. **Compassion.** Compassion is unconditional love and empathy. It's understanding that you and your partner are two humans doing the best you can.

2. **Trust.** Both partners trust they can go to the other. Both partners trust that the other's love is unconditional.

3. **Honesty.** Honesty is the foundation of that deeper level of closeness. You can tell your partner your deepest secrets and trust they will still love you unconditionally.

4. **Communication.** As you get more comfortable sharing things with your partner, intimacy naturally develops.

5. **Affection.** You can develop that closeness from intimacy through physical affection. Affection can be shown in different ways, like hugs, kisses and cuddles.

6. **Mutual Responsibility.** Building intimacy will take work, commitment, and responsibility from both partners. **There will be some days where one partner will need to carry more responsibility than the other.** Overall, there should be a mutual commitment to getting closer.

**All the work you put in to build intimacy will be worth it.** You will feel closer to your partner than ever before.

# 9 Obstacles to Building Intimacy

Intimacy requires love, time, and care. It can be watered like a plant – but in order to grow, this plant needs to be watered by both partners. It takes two to tango.

Getting to know each other and building closeness sounds easy. But the reality is that humans are not perfect. **The path to intimacy will have obstacles and roadblocks.**

Some men have trouble building intimacy because they fear losing their sense of independence. On the other hand, some women can have trouble with intimacy because they focus on fixing their partner rather than accepting their partner.

Obstacles like that can show up and stand in the way of true intimacy. When you notice the obstacles show up, remember the reason why you started the relationship in the first place.

Remembering why you love your partner will help keep you going as you overcome these obstacles to building intimacy together.

## Avoid or remove these obstacles:

1. **Trapping yourself in routine.** Your relationship might reach a point where everything becomes routine. You find yourself at the same restaurants, repeating conversations, doing the same weekend activities. **Getting trapped in that routine can plateau the level of intimacy you have with your partner.**

   ● Surprise your partner with a date in a new location.
   ● Choose a new hobby to pick up together.

2. **Building walls.** During an argument, you might have the tendency to shut down and stop communicating with your partner. If that happens, step away, take a break and return to the conversation later.

   ● Calmly let your partner know that you need a break from the conversation.

- Take a 20–30–minute break.

- Revisit the conversation with your partner.

3. **Fear of intimacy.** A subconscious fear of intimacy can prevent you from getting closer to your partner. You might have difficulty communicating your own needs or have a tendency to sabotage the relationships you enter.

   - Identify where the fear comes from. Are you scared of being hurt?
   - Set boundaries to feel safe.
   - Communicate your feelings.

4. **Lack of time.** You might find yourself prioritizing other things above your relationship. If you struggle with time, pay attention to what's been prioritized above the relationship.

   - Schedule regular date nights and times to check in with your partner.

5. **Dishonesty.** True intimacy cannot be built if there are secrets or dishonesty in a relationship. Dishonesty might show up from a fear of the closeness and vulnerability that comes from honesty. If this is the case for you, **keep in mind that honesty will bring you closer to your partner.**

   ● Be transparent with your feelings.
   ● Create a safe space for both of you to share uncomfortable truths.

6. **Aggression.** Aggression might indicate a lack of respect in the relationship. Being aggressive, critical, or showing contempt is a flag that should be taken seriously.

   • **Build a culture of appreciation.** Go out of your way to let your partner know how much you appreciate them.

7. **Doubtfulness or lack of trust.** Couples might have a hard time trusting because of something happened in the past or something their partner has done. **It's important to address any lack of trust because intimacy is unobtainable without it.**

8. **Control.** Sometimes we subconsciously try to control what happens in the relationship or how our partner feels. This can be an obstacle to intimacy. We have to let go of our desire to control in order to experience true intimacy.

9. **Avoidance.** Maybe you want to avoid a topic that needs to be addressed or avoid having a difficult conversation. This will be an obstacle to intimacy.

You might notice these obstacles are very human! They will pop up and occur naturally. Do your best to be cognizant of them and remove them from your relationship.

**When you remove these obstacles and follow the exercises in this book, you can experience the love and joy possible from true, deep intimacy.**

# Self-Intimacy and its Impact on the Relationship

"A problem in a relationship is often actually a personal problem requiring personal work." – David Richo

To build a truly healthy, intimate relationship, start with your relationship with yourself.

When you have a healthy relationship with yourself, you trust yourself more, find it easier to empathize with your partner, and are able to communicate your needs.

When you know your wants and needs, you can work with your partner to create a shared set of rules in your relationship. If one or both partners don't know what they need, things get overlooked. And that's where resentment comes to play.

Sometimes, when our relationship with ourselves is unhealthy, we project our fantasies onto our partner. This leads to obstacles to building intimacy, like trying to manipulate or control our partner. It can also lead to having unrealistic expectations and being disappointed when they are not met.

When you have a healthy relationship with yourself, you don't project fantasies or unrealistic expectations on your partner.

**A healthy relationship with yourself also means you feel emotions without letting them control your behavior.** This will make it easier for you to make wiser decisions and understand your partner.

An unhealthy relationship with yourself may stem from low self-esteem. When you have low self-esteem, you depend on your partner in different ways in order to feel happy. While it's fine for our partner to be a source of our happiness, we shouldn't depend on that source.

**The goal is to build your own source of esteem** so that you know how to make yourself happy.

Just like you schedule in time to spend with your partner, schedule time to spend with yourself.

## Follow these tips to improve your relationship with yourself:

1. **Prioritize your routine and things you love.** What things did you enjoy before you entered the relationship? What parts of your routine are most important to your happiness and well-being?

2. **Schedule a date with yourself once per week.** See the date with yourself as a way to keep the relationship with your

partner healthy too.

3. **Focus on what you can control.** Sometimes we get so focused on controlling an outcome instead of letting things happen. Learn to focus on what you can control to strengthen your positivity and relationship with yourself.

4. **Speak up for yourself.** Practice speaking up for yourself and communicating your needs to your partner and others.

5. **Take responsibility.** If you do something that hurts someone else, or make a mistake, take responsibility for it. **That honesty will show that you have a deep sense of pride and good intention.**

- When you take responsibility for your actions, you can also learn more about yourself and you can learn from your mistakes.

- Get curious: "What does this situation bring out in me?"

● Avoid criticizing yourself. But think about how you could have done or said something differently.

6. **Check in with yourself.** Regularly check-in with yourself. Do you feel resentful lately? Why do you think that is? Do you feel happy lately? Why?

# Building Trust and Intimacy

Build trust as the foundation for your relationship's intimacy. With trust, you know you can turn to your partner for support. **You trust that your partner's love is unconditional.**

The trust is built without projections, expectations, or trying to control the other person.

Trust is built by being reliable and showing up to the relationship as a teammate.

You can also let David Richo's Five A's of Love guide your journey of building trust in your relationship.

## Build Trust with These Five A's of Love

These Five A's of Love can help you build trust, intimacy, and long-lasting love. Integrate them into your routine and give them to your relationship regularly.

1. **Attention.** Connect and give your partner attention.

2. **Acceptance.** Accept your partner as they are instead of trying to change them or judge them.

3. **Appreciation.** Create a culture of appreciation as an alternative to aggression or resentment.

4. **Affection.** Give your partner affection unconditionally.

5. **Allowing.** Let go of any nature to control your partner. Allow your partner to be free.

Check-in with your partner. Are these Five A's of Love a part of your relationship routine?

## Other Ways to Build Trust

Building trust is one of the foundational parts to deepen intimacy. Trust is built by being reliable and showing up over time.

## Here are other ways to build trust:

1. **Keep agreements.** Be reliable. Show your partner that they can trust your word.

2. **Support your beloved.** This will show your partner that they can rely on you for support.

3. **Take care of yourself, but never at the expense of your partner or others.** This will show your partner that you are not their responsibility but their partner.

4. **Respect each other's boundaries.** We have boundaries that show others how we are willing to be treated. Avoiding stepping over established lines shows both compassion and respect.

5. **Listen without judgment.** This will create a safe space in the relationship.

# What to Do if Trust is Broken

You might reach a point where trust in the relationship gets broken. This can happen when one partner shuts the other down, breaks a promise, or becomes unreliable. It can also happen if someone deceives, lies, or even cheats on the other.

**Trust is an essential part of intimacy. If trust gets broken, it needs to be fixed.** Both partners will need to commit to rebuilding trust in the relationship.

**It takes an effort from both sides to rebuild trust.**

**If trust has been broken, here's where to start:**

1. **Look within first.** This self-reflection will be difficult, but it's important to face.

   ● Why did this issue occur? If you hid something from your partner, why did you hide it? If you cheated on your partner, why?

● Where is the problem? What is behind the problem?

2. **Be completely honest with your partner.** To build trust and intimacy, one must be open and honest with their partner. Share with them what you learned about yourself and your needs during the self-reflection process.

3. **Apologize sincerely.** If you broke the trust, show that you understand what went wrong, acknowledge that you hurt your partner, and promise you will not repeat the behavior. **Be true to your word.**

4. **Be compassionate about how your partner feels.** When trust is broken, repair will need to be done. Be patient and compassionate. Hold space for your partner and how they were feeling.

5. **Resolution.** Talking through a resolution will give both of you clear goals about a way forward.

● What does each partner need?

● What are the next steps of resolution? For example, a
   next step might be individual or couple's therapy. Or a
   commitment to changing behavior.

● Is there anything that was left out?

6. **Rebuild trust.** Rebuilding trust after a partner broke it can be
   difficult. Instead of building trust through a history of actions,
   **learn how to rebuild trust based on your partner's word.**

● Another way to build intimacy and trust is a "willingness
   to work out problems" (such as how comfortable do you
   feel about talking about what is missing in the
   relationship & also what is fulfilling in the relationship?)

● **Be patient with the process because rebuilding trust
   takes time.**

# Emotional Intimacy

"To be fully seen by somebody, then, and be loved anyhow – this is a human offering that can border on miraculous." – Elizabeth Gilbert

Emotional intimacy is how safe and secure you feel with your partner. It's built through raw, deeper conversations about feelings, struggles, and needs.

Some people find it hard to build emotional intimacy. At first it seems easy to share your fears and your dreams. But sometimes as people get closer and closer, it gets harder to keep your walls down. **Letting someone in also means letting them see more of you, your fears and dreams.**

But getting closer to someone helps fulfill our human desire of feeling connected and strengthens our well-being. It feels incredible to be able to talk with your partner openly.

## Here's how to build emotional intimacy in your relationship:

1. **Practice naming feelings.** As you learn to name feelings, you might realize you don't have the vocabulary to do so.

   - Happy: Curious, respected, confident, playful, loving, thankful
   - Surprised: Amazed, excited, shocked, dismayed, eager
   - Bad: Stressed, indifferent, pressured, unfocused, busy, embarrassed
   - Fearful: Insecure, scared, rejected, worthless
   - Angry: frustrated, disappointed, jealous, annoyed, furious, skeptical

● Sad: Lonely, hurt, vulnerable, isolated, powerless, fragile

2. **Validate your partner's feelings.** Listen openly and validate your partner's feelings to create that safe space for each other to share.

3. **Be curious.** Ask open-ended questions. When your partner shares something uncomfortable with you, **ask questions to help process the experience.**

4. **Listen with empathy.** Any conversation where someone doesn't feel heard will create distance. Pause to hear, listen, and understand what your partner is feeling. **Nod to show your partner you're engaged and present.**

5. **Share.** Share what you're going through and feeling as well.

Emotional intimacy is based on equal trust, curiosity, and engagement. Be curious about your partner and be willing to open yourself up as well. You'll both be rewarded with greater feelings of intimacy.

# Intellectual Intimacy

While emotional intimacy is grown by communicating feelings and needs, intellectual intimacy is grown by discussing opinions.

Intellectual intimacy is getting to know how your partner's mind works. **It's hearing your partner's ideas, thoughts, and opinions.** You grow intellectual intimacy by discussing in–depth topics like society, politics, or lifestyle choices.

You understand what beliefs and values guide your partner's decision–making.

You don't have to agree on everything intellectually. But there does need to be a level of mutual respect. **Even if you disagree with your partner, you accept their opinion and respect them for it.**

## Tips to build intellectual intimacy:

1. **Listen to understand.** Understand where your partner's opinions come from. Think about how the way they were raised, or their experiences, might shape their beliefs. **Let go of any need to be right.**

2. **Discuss something you've read recently.** Talk about your takeaways from the reading and ask your partner what they think. Explore different ideas together.

3. **If you disagree with your partner, do so respectfully.** Entertain opinions and consider ideas.

4. **Discuss lifestyle choices with your partner. This can also be spiritual intimacy.**

- What are your life goals?

- Do you want to raise children?

- How do you feel about marriage?

- What is your life purpose?

5. **Accept.** Accept your partner, their beliefs, and their opinions.

Remember that intimacy is built on acceptance. It's okay to disagree with your partner – you have to be willing to accept each person as they are.

Following the steps above will help you build intellectual intimacy and mutual respect.

# Building Physical Intimacy

You get closer to your partner through physical affection like hugs, cuddles, and touching.

Just like you can have intimacy without sex, you can have sex without intimacy. To build physical intimacy, be curious about how touching can bring you and your partner closer.

**Being touched feels good – but there are other health benefits, too!**

# Read these other health benefits of physical intimacy:

1. Lower levels of cortisol

2. Boost your immune system

3. Helps you live longer

4. Keeps you happier

5. Increased oxytocin (a soothing hormone)

6. Less loneliness

7. Lower blood pressure

# Try these exercises to build physical intimacy:

1. **Eye–gazing.** Stare into your partner's eyes for a few minutes. This is a tantric exercise that will bring you closer together.

2. **Touch your partner.** Reach your hand out to touch your partner on the shoulder. Find ways to touch your partner and remind them physically that you care.

3. **Hold hands.** Hold hands with your partner over a coffee or while you're out walking.

4. **Schedule sex.** It might feel unnatural to schedule time for physical intimacy, but with busy schedules **it shows that you put the physical connection with your partner as a priority.**

5. **Cuddle.** At the end of a long day, simply cuddle with your partner.

6. **Give each other massages.** Taking time to give the other massages can be a relaxing and connecting experience for you both.

**In addition to feeling great, physical intimacy on a regular basis boosts your immune system, helps you live longer, and keeps you happier.**

And you can build that physical closeness through more than just sex. It's about the closeness between you and your partner physically.

# Experiential Intimacy

Experiential intimacy is built by doing shared activities with your partner. It's growing your memory bank, creating inside jokes, and enjoying time together.

**When you do something new together, you can recreate that spark you felt at the beginning of your relationship.**

Building experiential intimacy can be simple because the only obstacle is finding the quality time to share with your partner.

Experiential intimacy can be grown through simple things like getting involved in activities together. Shake up your routine and do something different with your partner!

## Ideas to build shared experiences with your partner:

1. Solve a puzzle together.
2. Read the same book.

3. Go on a walk or hike.

4. Dance.

5. Exercise together.

6. Travel somewhere new.

7. Try a different restaurant.

8. Cook a new dish.

9. Take a painting class.

10.     Watch a movie.

11. Sit in the garden.

12.     Go bicycling.

13.     Take an improv class.


**Show your partner that they are a priority to you by doing these activities without technology.** Put away your phones or even implement "no-phone" areas at home.


Schedule the time and effort to do something new with your partner.

# Building Intimacy Beyond Conflict

"Understanding someone's suffering is the best gift you can give another person. Understanding is love's other name. If you don't understand, you can't love." – Thich Nhat Hanh

Have you ever watched an argument between you and your partner turn into two monologues where both of you are talking, but neither is listening?

Building intimacy and falling in love feels easy. Knowing how to keep the love alive does not feel as natural.

It's easy to either give up on the relationship when things get hard or settle because you love your partner.

**Remember that disagreements are unavoidable. What you can control is the way you respond to conflict.** Instead of settling when things get hard, the disagreements you have can become a way for you to understand each other better, learn, and grow.

When you learn how to build intimacy beyond conflict, you'll see that the content of the disagreements isn't what's most important. You'll see how behind the content, what matters is:

- The way you respond
- What your triggers/patterns are
- How you resolve the conflict
- Respond with honesty and openness!
- The relationship is more important than a need to be right
- Listening can be a demonstration of love

## Here's What You Can Learn About Communication in Conflict

The Gottman Institute uses The Four Horsemen as a metaphor to describe communication styles that predict the end of a relationship.

To build closeness with your partner, discuss The Four Horsemen. Talk about how these communication styles have shown up for you in the past or present.

Think about the arguments you've had with your partner or others. **What is the default way you respond?**

Disagreements are a natural part of relationships. You might find yourself responding to an argument in one of these four ways.

**Implement the techniques below to help you manage your own feelings, learn more about your partner, and build trust in the relationship:**

1. **Criticism.** Criticism shows up as an attack on your partner's character.

   - **Express a positive need.** Use an "I" statement to talk about how you are feeling and what you need to feel better.

2. **Contempt.** Contempt is criticism from a position of superiority. **It is a level beyond criticism and the greatest predictor of divorce.** Contempt shows up as comments that make one partner seem superior to the other.

   - **Build a "culture of appreciation."** Integrate it into your routine to express affection, gratitude, and appreciation for your partner.

3. **Defensiveness.** Defensiveness is a reversal or deflection of blame. While defensiveness comes from trying to protect yourself, it has the potential to escalate the conflict.

   - **Take responsibility.** Even if you only accept responsibility for part of the conflict, you can admit your role and work towards a compromise.

4. **Stonewalling.** Stonewalling is when one partner completely withdraws from the conversation.

- **Take a break. Research has found that couples who take a 30-minute break during an argument return to the discussion in a more productive way.** When you feel overwhelmed, ask for at least 20 minutes so you can both distract yourselves from the conversation and calm down.

**The way you resolve disagreements with your partner can save your relationship.**

At the end of the conversation, revisit the reasons why you started the relationship in the first place. It was probably because you and your partner wanted to support each other's growth.

**Ask your partner how you can support them.**

You will not always agree with each other. But you can both learn how to manage those uncomfortable feelings during a disagreement.

# 5 Exercises to Build Intimacy

Building intimacy in your relationship requires training, too. Some of these exercises might feel tedious at first but try to trust the process.

**Use these activities to deepen the intimacy in your relationship and understand your partner in a way you haven't before:**

1. **Do something new together.** When you do something new together, you recreate that spark you felt at the beginning of your relationship. Shake up your routine and do something new and exciting.

    ● Take a cooking class.

- Go on a new hike somewhere new.

- Book a staycation.

- Go on a walk nearby and point out new things you notice.

- Pack a picnic.

- Exercise together.

- Dance.

2. **Ask these questions.** Sharing personal information between you and your partner can help build intimacy. **Set aside a time where you and your partner can sit down and ask each other these questions to deepen your connection.**

- How do you think you have grown in the past five years?

- How do you want to grow in the next five years?

- What are three qualities you admire about yourself?

- What is something you've always wanted to do, but haven't done yet? Why not?

- Tell me about one of the happiest days of your life.

- What is one of the most embarrassing moments of your life?

- What's your fondest childhood memory?

- Which small romantic gestures would you like more of?

- Tell me about what the perfect career looks like to you.

- What traits do you value in a friend?

- What do you need to feel happy and fulfilled?

● How is sexuality contributing to your intimacy and bringing you closer together?

3. **Discover your partner's love language.** Gary Chapman identified five ways that people give and receive love. To deepen the closeness between you and your partner, learn each other's love language. This way, you can learn how to communicate with your partner in his or her love language.

   - **Words of Affirmation.** Do you or your partner receive love through words? If so, the best way to communicate would be to acknowledge your partner using kind words, compliments, and words of appreciation.

   - **Quality Time.** With a love language of quality time, spending meaningful time together means the most to that person. The best way to communicate here would be to give your partner undivided attention, show you are listening, and do activities together.

- **Acts of Service.** Partners whose love language is acts of service believe that actions speak louder than words. Communicate love via acts of service by picking up some of your partner's chores when they are busy, making your partner breakfast, or giving your partner a massage.

- **Giving and Receiving Gifts.** People with the love language of gifts receive love by giving and receiving meaningful gifts. Communicate this love language by paying attention to what your partner values and finding a gift that reflects those values.

- **Touch.** When someone's love language is touch, they receive love through physical actions like holding hands, cuddling, and kissing. Communicate this love language by touching your partner while they are speaking, greeting them with a hug, or inviting them to cuddle.

4. **Check-in weekly.** Schedule a time to check-in with your partner. Be prepared to be open and honest! This means

telling your partner how feedback makes you feel (for example, maybe you feel embarrassed when they share what's missing from the relationship) instead of being defensive.

- How are you doing, really?
- What is missing from the relationship?
- How can I support your growth?

No matter how long you and your partner have been together, these exercises will always help you reignite the flame.

## Practice Intimacy in Your Daily Life

Small actions build up and compound over time.

**Think about these small actions as a way to pay into your relationship's "intimacy bank":**

1. **Respond to your partner's signals.** Notice when your partner reaches out to you. This might show up in simple ways, like a

smile or suggestion. Turn towards your partner for connection.

2. **Show and tell your partner you appreciate them.** To foster a culture of appreciation, tell your partner you appreciate them!

- "Thank you for helping with the dishes."
- "It means a lot to me that you listen."
- "I appreciate how supportive you are."

3. **Be affectionate to your partner based on their love language.**

- Compliment the way they look or say, "I love you."
- Give one another a massage.
- Set aside quality time to do an activity together.
- Surprise your partner with a thoughtful gift, like a flower you picked up on your way home from work.
- Do some of their chores around the house.

4. **Remember the small things.** Building intimacy doesn't always have to be time-consuming or complicated! **Even the small**

- Ask your partner how their day was.
- Be playful.
- **Do one act of kindness for your partner each day.**

Although it might feel unnatural or tedious at first to integrate these things into your daily routine, the extra work you do each day will help bring you and your partner closer together.

"I want to be in a relationship where you telling me you love me is just a ceremonious validation of what you

Building intimacy with your partner can be the way to rekindle the fire you felt at the beginning of the relationship. The happiest couples are those who have intentionally built on all four levels of intimacy.

**Intimacy is the most important way to nurture your relationship.** At the end of the day, a happy relationship doesn't come effortlessly or without work.

Set aside time to talk with your partner about the different levels of intimacy and what they mean to you. A healthy relationship will have all types of intimacy, but you can put extra effort into your partner's favorite level of intimacy.

When you build a truly intimate relationship, you will grow and thrive together.

On the next few pages, there will be a few questions to reflect on how to improve your relationship going forward.

# Increasing Loving Communication With Your Partner

● Do you devote your full attention to your partner when they're talking with you? How can you strengthen your listening skills?

● Do you laugh together each day? What can you do to bring

more humor and fun into your life?




● Do you share your hopes and dreams together? How will you

make them happen? Do you have a detailed plan? How can

you work towards these dreams each day?

● Do you follow through with your commitments to your partner?
Do you procrastinate in doing it? Why? Will a compromise
work better for you in a current commitment so that you can
always follow through?

● How do you currently handle disagreements? How can you
turn your disagreements into loving communication instead?

● Do you sweat the small stuff? How can you develop more patience and understanding for your differences?

● Are you open and honest with your partner, even in tough situations? How can you make your communications more honest?

● How do you communicate your love to your partner? Do you
  show your love numerous times each day? What else can you
  do to show your love and fulfill your partner's needs and
  desires?




● Do you schedule quality time together? What does quality
  time mean to you? What does it mean to your partner? How
  can you meet both of your needs for this time together?

# Healthy Relationship Habits Action Plan

It can be helpful to reminisce and reflect on your relationship to strengthen and reinforce your connection.

Storytelling is a great way to do this, but you may also want to write your responses in a journal and then discuss things from both perspectives.

Sit down together as a couple and answer one or two of these each evening for a week.

## Questions for Couple Sharing

- How do you show your love for each other in little ways and big ways?

●How do you divide tasks and household chores?

●Do you have an endearing term or "pet name" for each other?

●Is there a personality difference in your partner or spouse that you have learned to respect and affirm?

●What is one compromise you have made with one another?

●How often do you say or demonstrate, "I love you!"? What are some examples?

●What do you like to do together?

● What was one of your favorite dating or
anniversary celebrations?




● What was one of your favorite birthday, graduation,
or promotion celebrations?




● What has influenced your sensitivity to each
other's needs?


**Daily Practice**

Make a list of five special things your partner has done for you.  Share your lists with each other and do at least one of the things on the other's list before the next mentoring conversation.

An option would be to share three things you would like for him or her to do for you that are ways of demonstrating love to you.

Help one another by giving him or her a positive target at which to aim. "I really like it when you __________________________."

**Contact me for other ideas to strengthen your relationship: askcoachshina@gmail.com or visit www.wyshinawest.com for more tips and advice.**

# Couple Commitment Worksheet

**I.** List the most important things about your relationship that you want to preserve and protect.

    1.

    2.

    3.

**II.** Complete the following by listing specific <u>actions</u> that you would like to request of your partner or spouse to enhance your relationship.

I would like more. . .

    1.

    2.

    3.

I would like less. . .

    1.

    2.

    3.

**III.** Exchange worksheets with your partner/spouse. Read and discuss both of your responses to Parts I and II. In the space below, write the things that you are willing to do to enhance your relationship based on these requests. Write this on your partner's/spouse's worksheet.

In order to enhance our relationship, I agree to protect. . .

    1.

    2.

    3.

In order to enhance our relationship, I commit to. . .

    1.

    2.

3.


**IV.** Based on your agreement, spend a few minutes talking with your partner/spouse about your responses.


**Need help with your relationship? Contact me: askcoachshina@gmail.com or visit wyshinawest.com for more tips and advice.**


# OVERCOMING INFIDELITY

# SELF–REFLECTION

# WORKSHEET


1. Have I allowed my appearance to fall to the wayside? How so? (This DOES NOT condone your spouse cheating, that was their choice. It had NOTHING to do with your appearance. I ask this question because we typically feel good when we look good and if you have stopped making sure that you look good, you're

probably not feeling good either and to change that, take a

moment to be honest with yourself to see why)

_________________________________________________

_________________________________________________

_________________________________________________

_________________________________________________

2. What are the top 3 things my partner and I argue about?
Why?

_________________________________________________

_________________________________________________

_________________________________________________

_________________________________________________

_______________________________________________

_______________________________________________

_______________________________________________

3. Am I truly happy in this relationship? Why?

_______________________________________________

_______________________________________________

_______________________________________________

_______________________________________________

4. What has been putting a strain on our relationship? Do our jobs, families, friends, financial situation, or children increase our stress levels?

_______________________________________________

_______________________________________________

________________________________________

________________________________________

________________________________________

5. How did I find out that my partner was unfaithful? How did this hurt me?

________________________________________

________________________________________

________________________________________

________________________________________

________________________________________

6. How did my partner react when confronted with infidelity? How did their reaction make me feel?

7. Which activities help me relax when I start to feel anxious about my partner potentially cheating again?

8. Has my partner changed since I discovered their infidelity? If so, how? If not, how would I like them to change?

_______________________________________________

_______________________________________________

_______________________________________________

_______________________________________________

_______________________________________________

9. Do I purposely start arguments with my partner simply because I am angry about something they've done in the past? How can I improve my communication style?

_______________________________________________

_______________________________________________

_______________________________________________

10.  Which character traits do I love about my partner and why are they the right person for me?

We have reached the end darlings. How do you feel? You should be feeling proud of yourself because honey I am proud of YOU!  You did it! I know it was tough to work through all of those bad feelings, but you did it! If you haven't already be sure to check out books 1 and 2 of Love You series and be on the lookout for book 4. That is the FINAL BOOK so you know it will be amazing and so worth it. They can all be found at wyshinawest.com, use code LOVEWINS for a special discount. Other places include Amazon and Barnes and Noble.

Thank you for your support and be sure to let me know your thoughts. Now go be the awesome person that you are. Until next time. Coach Shina